SACRED GEOMETRY
CARDS
FOR THE VISIONARY PATH

"Francene Hart sees and paints what is glorious about life. She puts one into a space of timeless wonder. This deck is alive with light and will offer fulfillment to your soul when you use it."

SONDRA RAY, AUTHOR OF
ROCK YOUR WORLD WITH THE DIVINE MOTHER

"Amazing work . . . amazing cards by a highly gifted artist. These works of art are powerful triggers for accessing the mystical and unconscious aspects of the psyche. A wonderful tool for inner work and exploration."

"STARMAN" JOSEPH MINA,
ASTROLOGER AND COAUTHOR OF
MANIFESTING WITH THE LIGHT OF THE MOON

SACRED GEOMETRY
CARDS
FOR THE VISIONARY PATH

Francene Hart

Bear & Company
Rochester, Vermont

Bear & Company
One Park Street
Rochester, Vermont 05767
www.BearandCompanyBooks.com

Bear & Company is a division of Inner Traditions International

Library of Congress Cataloging-in-Publication Data
Hart, Francene, 1948–
  Sacred geometry cards for the visionary path / Francene Hart.
    p. cm.
  Summary: "A boxed set of cards and book, the sequel to Sacred Geometry Oracle Deck"—Provided by publisher.
  ISBN 978-1-59143-092-6
  1. Fortune-telling by cards. 2. Geometry—Miscellanea. I. Title.

BF1878.H36 2008
133.3'242—dc22
                                                                    2008014249

Printed and bound in China by Regent

10 9 8 7 6 5 4 3 2 1

Text design and layout by Jon Desautels
This book was typeset in Goudy Old Style

To send correspondence to the author of this book, mail a first-class letter to the author c/o Inner Traditions • Bear & Company, One Park Street, Rochester, VT 05767, and we will forward the communication.

With love and gratitude for the opportunity to further explore ancient and universal wisdom and create an evolving vision of a future we may consciously embrace.

With gratitude for guidance from Spirit and deep appreciation for the beloved friends who have supported me heart and soul in the manifestation of this oracle.

Mahalo nui loa Tutu Pele for the honor of living on your sacred slopes.

CONTENTS

INTRODUCTION

This journey into Sacred Geometry has taken me, and many of you, to places beyond where we might have imagined. Far past simple information about pattern and arc, this exploration has become a pilgrimage of the heart and an eloquent expression of universal wisdom. Sacred Geometry continues to amaze and surprise as insight and understanding come pouring in through this divine matrix of sacred configurations.

This second oracle deck reflects an increasing fascination with Sacred Geometry. For a growing number of individuals, its relevance has much to do with our awareness of and participation in conscious evolution. As we become ever more awake to the effects we have on our reality and that of the earth, the *Sacred Geometry Cards for the Visionary Path* provides encouragement and support.

As you gain awareness of how these shapes and configurations affect us on all levels—from microcosm to macrocosm—you will develop an appreciation of a divine plan that includes the amazing "Language of Light" called Sacred Geometry.

Sacred Geometry Cards for the Visionary Path merges powerful, evocative images with meaningful theories and creative wisdom. It both builds on and steps beyond the *Sacred Geometry Oracle Deck*, and the two sets of cards can be used together.

The sixty-four images are all from original watercolor paintings. They represent many years devoted to creating art, and their inspiration is derived from several continents and beyond. My paintings are inspired by nature, Spirit, cross-cultural links, a fascination with Sacred Geometry, and a trust that it is our path to move beyond the old paradigm of separation and fear to walk in the light of unity and PEACE.

I have known for several years that one of the purposes of my artmaking is to translate Spirit into material form. In some sense I feel like an interpreter or gatekeeper. I present you with this gift so that you may enjoy and grow in your own manner and find your own truth within the art and prose. You may discover that these images evoke personal impressions that go beyond the text or my original inspiration. Allow that they may have significance in your individual story, evoking additional dreams and visions.

Sacred Geometry and Beyond

I have been deeply heartened by the response to the *Sacred Geometry Oracle Deck* and am grateful to each and every one of you who have it in your collection. I hold that effort dear to my heart and know it will remain an important tool for strengthening our connection to the intelligence of the universe.

The original oracle was designed, at least in part, to fulfill a personal mission to create a wisdom system for those who have yet to discover the knowledge inherent in Sacred Geometry. The original cards include diagrams of geometrical configurations and rely on these to demonstrate an understanding of the concepts in conjunction with the art. In this new oracle you will find glyphs along with the card text that illustrate the geometry described therein.

I am constantly expanding my responsiveness to Sacred Geometry and am in a perpetual state of respect and awe at its relevance to our times. There are a few configurations considered Sacred Geometry that are not included in this deck. Please understand it is not out of disrespect or intentional omission. The sixty-four images you see are the ones that wanted to reveal themselves for our mutual growth.

Why another deck? As I continue my pilgrimage into the heart of this wisdom, I see how immensely the interest in Sacred Geometry has grown in the past few years and recognize how hungry many are for additional information and vision. I have known for several years that another effort, an evolution, was in the wings, yet resisted it, preferring the simple life I have created in Hawaii. Still, this information kept knocking at the door and flowing through my paintings. Finally the call was too loud, and I could no longer refuse this sacred responsibility. Once I accepted this undertaking, the vision came pouring in and through me, offering assurance of its significance and timeliness. This evolution has been occasionally overwhelming and has fully consumed me—body, mind, and Spirit—during the gestation of this oracle.

It is with a deep sense of humility that I present to you *Sacred Geometry Cards for the Visionary Path*. For those just beginning this journey, I extend a warm welcome. There is much to be learned, enjoyed, and experienced.

May it bring you joy and inspire you to further adventures.

What Is Sacred Geometry?

Sacred Geometry is an ancient science, a sacred language, and a key to understanding the way the universe is designed. Sacred Geometry, in one form or another, has been studied throughout the world, since curiosity led to the exploration of relationships. It is the study of shape and form, wave and vibration, and moving beyond third-dimensional reality.

It is the "new science of compassion."

It is the language of creation that exists as the foundation of all matter, and it is a vehicle of Spirit. It has been called the "blueprint for all of creation," the "harmonic configuration of the soul," and the "divine rhythm that results in manifest existence."

At times kept secret, in mystery schools and secret societies, Sacred Geometry has become available in our time as a tool to aid in our movement toward conscious evolution. From the atom to our spiral DNA; from the geometric patterns into which cells divide to the energy fields within and around our bodies and the planet; from architecture to advertising—we are constructed of and influenced by geometry.

Often termed the "Language of Light," Sacred Geometry has the ability to balance and inform. The effects of this language are obvious when we journey to sacred sites. Have you visited a pyramid or medicine wheel? You have felt the effects. Have you walked a labyrinth, participated in a spiral dance, or constructed a mandala? You have felt the effects. Have you watched light dance through a crystal or been fascinated by looking through a microscope or a telescope? You have felt the effects.

From microcosm to macrocosm, from the first cell to the incomprehensible depths of the universe, patterns gather and repeat in confirmation of our connectedness. When we recognize these geometric archetypes and their relationship to the underlying structure of the universe, we see clearly that there is no separation. We are physically and spiritually ONE.

Conscious Evolution and Its Connection to Sacred Geometry

Conscious evolution holds that humankind now realizes we have the power to affect and transform the path toward our future, both individually and collectively. Our visions and dreams, as surely as our actions, have an effect on our daily experience and our future. The inner life of the individual—including thoughts, attitudes, emotions, motivations, and spiritual experience—has an effect on the whole. It is our choice to make a difference.

Beyond the harrowing news of mainstream media and bleak predictions of some futurists, we find scientists, creative thinkers, and visionaries who walk the path of potential, optimistic that we may yet find solutions to the effects of the arrogance and fragility of our humanness. We have become powerful enough to make ourselves extinct, yet we also are becoming self-aware enough to chart our own destiny. We are a species of choice waking up to the truth of our interconnection.

Sacred Geometry meshes perfectly with the ideas of conscious evolution. The lattices of life force displayed through the geometries confirm our intimate relationship with All That Is. Conscious evolution holds the potential to guide our movement toward a future of our own design. Through conscious evolution and choice we will draw on compassion, intelligence, and creativity to engender all humanity with greater coherence and synergy and evolve the vision of a brilliant future.

Crop Formations

Several cards contain images borrowed from crop formations. The striking geometries created by the circle makers take us on an odyssey of pattern and design, revealing models for our enjoyment and speculation. Their origin is an inviting mystery.

My attraction to these glyphs and the intricacy of their patterns led me, in recent crop seasons, to include them in my paintings. It has been moving to experience the information manifesting through these crop formations. They have profoundly enlightened my art. It is with respect that I include the wisdom of the circle makers as part of this oracle. I invite you to explore this phenomenon for yourself.

Sunset Activation

The image that appears on the flip side of every card is called "Sunset Activation." This painting was inspired by a magnificent sunset that displayed powerful contrasting elements in nature. "Sunset Activation" excites the mind and senses with storm clouds and rainbows coupled with golden spirals and other elements of Sacred Geometry.

This display of nature's different facets occurred at a sacred place, a pu'uhonua, known as the City of Refuge. In old Hawaii, a pu'uhonua was a place that protected and sheltered all who arrived. Those who broke a kapu, one of the ancient laws against the gods, could avoid certain execution by fleeing to the pu'uhonua. Safe haven was granted to all who reached its walls; however, restitution was required before reentering the community. This is a place of shelter and forgiveness. This vision is an evocative place of refuge.

An intricate formation borrowed from a crop circle is embedded in the center of the image. It is thought to be a combination of Egyptian and Mayan glyphs. My intent was to work with this formation and explore how its essence might enlighten my artmaking. Several times while painting I felt as if I was being thrust through time. This feels appropriate—the Mayans are revered as master timekeepers.

See how this Sunset Activation stimulates your awareness. Allow the geometry and symmetry of nature to pull you into this image and support you visionary path.

Suggestions for Reading the Cards

You may wish to consult this oracle in various ways. Choosing one card is a great way to begin and offers an instant reading. A simple way to make your choice is to hold the deck and handle the cards as you focus on a question or intention. Combining your awareness and the intelligence of your heart with the wisdom system contained in the oracle will determine which card or cards you choose. Handle the cards. Shuffle them if you wish, or spread them before you face down and move your hands across the sixty-four choices until one seems to stick to your fingers. Another method is to cut the cards a few times and then choose the top one. Refer to the text to find your message by looking up the number on the card. Use the same procedure for any of the spreads. While pulling a spread, if a certain aspect needs further clarification, choose another card and lay it on top of the first. This may offer you additional insight into your inquiry.

Feel free to invent your own spreads. Simply ask from your core essence and assign qualities that feel relevant. Listen to the oracle's counsel yet take to heart only the guidance that rings true for you.

Reversed Cards

If you pull a card upside down from the deck, you may have encountered a reversed aspect. This indicates a challenge but should not be considered bad. In this oracle the reversed aspects are very simple and are more cautionary than predictive. You are asked to see them as another facet of the information presented with the card.

Using *Sacred Geometry Cards for the Visionary Path* with the *Sacred Geometry Oracle Deck*

You may discover additional information by using this oracle in conjunction with the *Sacred Geometry Oracle Deck.* There are various ways to approach this. The simplest is to choose one card from each deck for any query you are making. Remember, the first deck informs almost as a teacher, presenting instruction while helping to develop your awareness of Sacred Geometry. *Sacred Geometry Cards for the Visionary Path* moves a step beyond, offering more stimulating visual images and encouraging your personal intuition to play a greater role. You are asked first and foremost to trust your intuition and "feel" how these images and words affect your body, mind, and Spirit.

Note: The spreads contained herein follow familiar geometry used in the first deck while adding an evolutionary outlook to aid your visionary pursuit.

Synergy Spread

Synergy is a mutually advantageous conjunction wherein the whole is greater than the sum of the parts. It is a dynamic state in which combined action is favored over the sum of individual component actions. Using the configuration called the Vesica Piscis, we find an ideal three-card spread for discovering insights into the synergy of ideas and how they may benefit your situation. You may also consider this a way of allowing for synergy between the right and left sides of your brain.

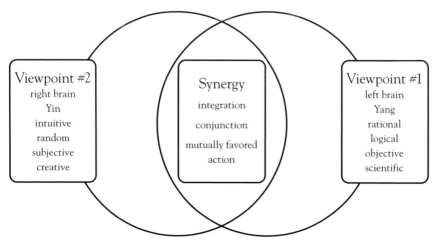

7

- First, choose a card with your right hand, representing one viewpoint or, interestingly, the function of your left brain, which is logical, rational, analytical, and objective. Use that portion of your reading to objectively look at the parts individually.
- Next, choose a card with your left hand to gain a second viewpoint, engaging the right side of your brain, which is random, intuitive, subjective and creative. Use that part of your reading to look at the whole.
- Finally, choose a card to represent the synthesis of ideas or viewpoints, where right and left brain can integrate and create something brand new. This is where the parts and the whole combine, creating synergy.

Earth in Balance Spread

As long there has been Earth, there has been a plan for Earth-ness, which values the planet as a living organism. Plants, animals, and humans need the support of a balanced Earth to be inspired and able to respond appropriately, ensuring not only survival but the good of all. Beliefs swing between serious alarm and indifference regarding the state of the world's natural environment, and between hope and despair concerning the condition of the inhabitants of our planet. This spread articulates your desire for balance both for our Mother Earth and for your personal well-being and happiness. Choose four cards moving left to right as you envision a life of balance.

This moment in Earth's story	Call to action continuous improvment	Sustainability	Hope for the future

- First, choose a card that represents where you stand today. Are you living this moment in balance, developing a vision of planetary and personal well-being?
- Second, select a card to denote a call to action. How might you act with heart to bring greater balance and continuous improvement to your own life and to all of Mother Earth?

- Next, choose a card symbolizing sustainability. This signifies your intent to provide the best outcome for yourself and in a larger sense for the human and natural environment both now and into the future.
- Finally, choose a card that will exemplify hope for the future and suggest how you may participate in the vision of Earth in Balance.

Conscious Choice Spread

Enhancing your ability to make up your mind, fully live in the present, and embrace your future with confidence and purpose are the principles of this spread. As you more fully realize who you are and consciously decide where you are going, you will expand an awareness of what is possible and attract more synchronicity and meaning into your life. This is an excellent spread for developing your capacity to understand how the choices you make when you are mindful and attentive are more lucid and unmistakable.

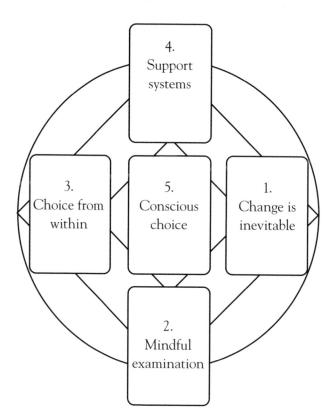

1. **Change is inevitable.** We all know this saying. Realizing that we influence the way change moves through our days strengthens our ability to move gracefully through life's meandering patterns. Ask how you may be guided as you contemplate choices.

2. **Mindful examination.** Be attentive to the situation and carefully research and assess the information as it presents itself. Are you considering how this choice will affect your loved ones as well as your own well-being?

3. **Choice from within.** Look inside and ask your inner guidance to help in the decision-making process. What advice emanates from your core?

4. **Support systems and external factors.** How may you engage the support of friends and colleagues both in helping facilitate your decision-making process and offering a hand once your choice becomes manifest?

5. **Conscious choice.** After all things are considered, you will be accountable to yourself and perhaps others for the choices you are considering. Ask this final card for a message of confirmation. Confidently, consciously choose.

Evolving the Dream Spread

The evolution of consciousness calls you to create a vision and utilize your imagination and farsightedness to bring about the manifestation of your dreams. This spread aptly suggests the geometry of the star tetrahedron to set your vision in motion and acts as a vehicle to help you visualize the aspects and their positive outcome. The Merkaba is composed of two interpenetrating tetrahedrons.

~Upward-Facing Tetrahedron~

1. **Begin with inspiration.** This is the spark that ignites your vision. This could be your grandest ambition wanting to take form. It may also be your humblest assignment presenting its unassuming face.

2. **Ask for guidance.** Asking for guidance will assist you in more completely understanding the course needed and in moving forward with the vision you have agreed to embrace.

3. **Resolve to act.** As you begin to evolve your dream, you will require a plan of action to get things moving. How may you be informed and move gracefully through this phase?

~Downward-Facing Tetrahedron~

4. **Listen to your intuition.** Extend your thoughts and feelings into your undertaking, instinctually perceiving the path that lies before you. What message does intuition offer?
5. **Nurture your vision.** It may take time and effort to evolve the expression of your dreams. Know that as you nurture your dreams you support the realization of your purpose.
6. **Manifestation.** What will it take to bring it all together? The final card indicates the outcome and asks you to be gentle with yourself as you bring this energy into and through your life and offer it to the world.

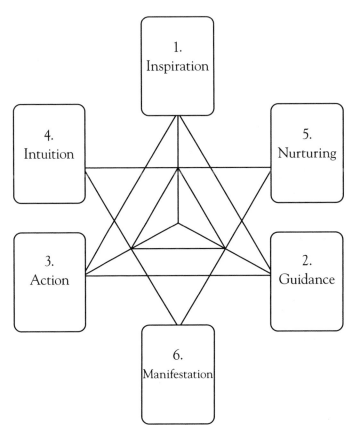

Seed of Life Spread

The Seed of Life has proven itself to be one of the most powerful patterns for observing the growth of projects, business, and all manner of relationships. It speaks of the seeding of ideas and expansion of new energy. This spread may also be helpful in understanding and processing challenges once a project or relationship is in progress.

Suggestion: Try pulling cards with a loved one or potential business partner. Observe your energy working together as you mutually confer with the oracle.

The Seed of Life is represented by six circles around a center circle. It is one of the glyphs associated with the Flower of Life.

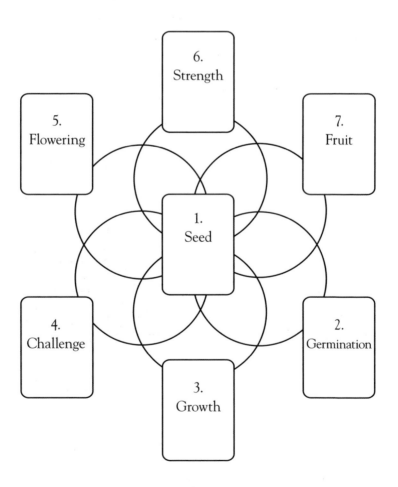

1. **In the center is the object of your inquiry.** It is the seed of your plan and holds the potential for ideas, enterprises, and new beginnings. Whether you are starting a business venture or falling in love, the seed is the beginning and holds within it infinite possibilities.

2. **Germination is action.** What will it take to germinate your creative ideas? This may represent the planning stages of a business venture. If your inquiry is about a relationship, this action is the sprouting stage when all is new and fragile. Care for this germination with tenderness and integrity.

3. **Growth is dynamic action.** Development is the focus of this card. It indicates movement toward your evolving vision: enacting that business plan, enrolling in classes, or signing up for that long-anticipated pilgrimage tour. In love, it is the time of blissful exploration and opening of the heart. Allow this card to inform that growth.

4. **Every venture has its challenges.** Recognizing this truth provides you with the means to face these challenges and grow from the lessons they offer. Don't avoid this aspect. Face obstacles and fears head-on so that they will have no power to derail you later.

5. **Flowering is the culmination of attention and intention.** When love flowers and business flourishes, we see the beauty of a plan coming together. The truth of the matter and the best outcome are revealed. Use this card to see how your efforts will flower.

6. **Strength is empowerment.** This is the place of power that comes from the heart. It is power to, not power over. Seek how you may cultivate the strength of your abilities. Ask how you might encourage the strength of others.

7. **The fruit is food for body and soul.** Experience how the seed you are planting will develop and bear fruit. This card reveals the maturation of plans and ideas. It speaks of growth and love fulfilled. Ask your heart to see achievement and harmony.

Spiraling Visions Spread

The proportions of the golden spiral represent the building blocks of creation. From quarks to quasars, creation spirals into existence using a code that is conveyed through this beautiful spiral. It speaks of cosmic order coupled with patterns of moving energy and change.

Golden spirals are related to the transcendental Phi ratio and a series called the Fibonacci numbers, in which each number is the sum of the two before it: 1, 1, 2, 3, 5, 8, 13, 21, 34, 55, 89 . . . This spread starts at the center, your core heart space, using the number eight as the key. Feel free to apply another of the Fibonacci numbers or move from the cosmic (outer) in toward the core spiraling vortex. Keep in mind that it is your intention and attention that will aid you in choosing the appropriate cards.

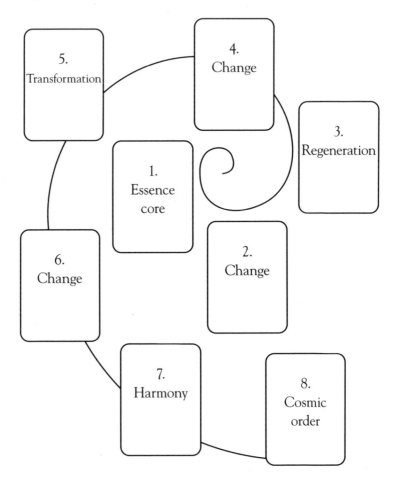

1. **Begin at your center.** Feel your heart and the heart of your inquiry as you ask what is crucial to this essence.

2. **Change.** As your vision begins to take form it will require you to make a number of changes. How might you enhance the positive aspects of change?

3. **Regeneration.** Challenging and timely, your vision requires your full participation. This could take a lot of energy. You may well feel a need to renew, restore, and rejuvenate. How might you engage this process of regeneration?

4. **Change.** As you consciously move with this spiral energy, you will encounter elements that may require you to correct your course or modify the way you view your progress. Is there an option you have not yet considered? Open your awareness to more change.

5. **Transformation.** How may you be advised at this juncture? What direction will your transformation take?

6. **Change.** Expect change as you flow with this purest form of moving energy. Learn to understand change is the way of nature. Do not fear its implications; rather, intend to fully feel this movement toward conclusion.

7. **Harmony.** The golden spiral speaks of harmony and accord. This card represents unity and agreement with divine purpose.

8. **Cosmic order.** As you move beyond the small world you inhabit, ask for affirmation of the divine working in your life, creating cosmic order.

The Cards

1. One Drop

Calm amid Chaos

In accordance with unity and Spirit, the circle represents a beginning that has no end. It is ever-expanding potential and represents our connection with the holographic nature of oneness.

We live in a world that at times feels overpowering and chaotic. It is easy to get caught up in a wild ride of emotional waves that feel as if they are out of your control, about to crash in upon you. Quantum physics views matter as a wave structure of space reality that is both continuous and discrete, both local and nonlocal. Sometimes it is all too much to handle.

You are the "one drop" that sits in the center of this circle and of your own reality. It is within this quiet place that you have the potential to experience calm amid the chaos of modern-day existence.

Choosing this card suggests that you enter the golden circle and feel its potential. Create for yourself a place of calm where you may be quiet. Meditate and remove yourself from the demands that consume your time and aggravate your emotional, physical, mental, and spiritual bodies. Remove yourself for a while from the chaos. Allow a knowing that in this still, calm place, "one drop" is all there is. View the rest of your life from this relaxed, tranquil, composed place.

I have one small drop
Of knowing in my soul
Let it dissolve in your ocean

RUMI

Reversed

This card has no reversed aspect.

2. Phase Mandala

Cycles • Movement

Living in cooperative balance with movement through cycles is the message of this card. We watch the moon as she rolls around the earth and shows us the faces of her phases. We experience the cycles of nature in the turning of the seasons and the phases of matter as solid, liquid, and gas. We cycle from childhood to adult to midlife to elder with the movement of our humanness.

Conception, manifestation, completion—everything moves in cycles and then begins anew. Mindful advancement through phases gives personal symbolic meaning to any event. Look to the underlying energy and movement rather than the actual event. On some level, a physical move, a new job or creative project, a birth, or an expansion in relationship is similar energetically. Each involves your intention to move toward new possibilities and fruition of your personal dream. Each represents a phase in the cycles of your life experience and spiritual growth. Each moves you toward the evolution of your vision.

Honor the progression of movement in your current situation.

Reversed

Realize you may not be able to reverse phases; however, you can move with them.

Francene Hart

3. The Kiss

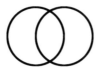

Earthly Love • Relationship

Beauty and love surround this sweet kiss. It takes place in the shared space where two interlocking golden rings create a Vesica Piscis. The almond-shaped or, viewed from another angle, eye-shaped center here symbolizes sacred space in which "The Kiss" becomes a union of souls. This symbolic joining celebrates the coming together of whole individuals in mutual understanding, finding common ground. Love expands through this shared vision. Further represented are the marriage of heaven and earth, of light and dark, and of elemental forces. A rainbow ring and one of stars entwine with the gold and suggest that as we come together in tenderness and respect, we also entwine with universal energies. Relationships can inspire communion that offers us the eyes to see beyond everyday reality into realms through which we may more clearly experience our connection to All That Is.

This card invites you to take a holistic view of the relationships in your life. See them existing in balance and respect. Look deeply into the eyes of each of your relationships, be they intimate or casual, for business or for any of the ways we interact with and teach each other. Feel how love feeds you and remember that nourishment, even when your friends are not around. Know that you also share a sacred union with your own heart. Offer yourself the love and respect that you seek from others. Connecting with the "feeling" of the kiss may take you to a heart space from which to heal old wounds and envision a bright future.

Reversed

The rings are off center or possibly disconnected altogether. Look with the intelligence of your heart for what it will take to be again in the doorway of understanding. Use the Vesica Piscis to symbolize realigning relationship.

4. Earth Prayers

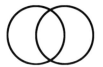

Stewardship • Sustainability

Embedded in this card is complex geometry that begins as the Flower of Life then transforms into tetrahedral patterns forming a protective divine matrix around the planet. From the birth portal at the center of the Vesica Piscis, our home, Mother Earth, shines in beauty and grace. Many colored hands surround and reside within these patterns, symbolizing participation of all beings in stewardship and sustainability.

Stewardship denotes understanding that there is Spirit in everything and that everything is connected. It implies awareness that each of our actions, whether it is growing a vegetable, cutting a tree, or using natural resources, affects the whole. Even our thoughts have this power. Being stewards of the earth doesn't mean living without abundance or placing judgment on the actions of others or ourselves. It does mean living with a sense of connectedness and relationship with all beings and respect for the earth.

Several indigenous tribes believe we must consider the effects of all our actions and demonstrate stewardship to the seventh generation. How might your daily actions and decisions be affected as you consider their effects seven generations into the future? As you consider this question and feel the tenderness of this time in Earth's story, realize also the power of your prayers and intentions. See and "feel" the earth as abundant and self-sustaining. See and "feel" humans treading lightly upon her land and making decisions that will defend rather than wound the earth. How can you more fully live with an attitude of stewardship?

Reversed
Apathy and lack of foresight cloud your decisions. Consciously return to an attitude of stewardship and begin again to live your prayers.

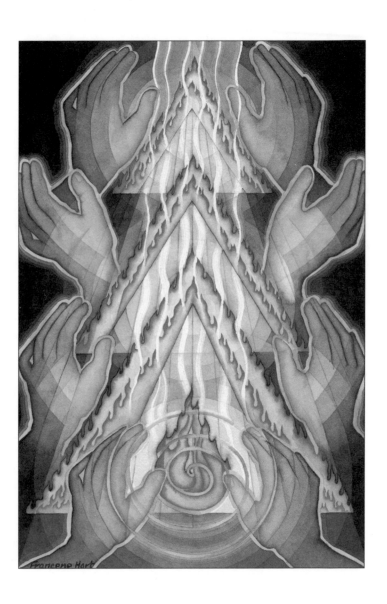

Francene Hart

5. Fire Keepers

Sacred Responsibility • Service

Fire is historically the source of protective warmth, light in the darkness, and heat for cooking and was essential to the survival of original
peoples. Firekeepers hold a sacred responsibility both for the physical survival and the ceremonial spiritual protection of the community. Theirs is
an essential and esteemed service.

Triangles represent Spirit, divinity, life, strength, harmony, and
completion. The upward-facing triangle is traditionally associated with
fire, action, and the masculine.

Three fires warming many hands invite you to warm to the understanding of these three levels of conscious personal mastery: physical
awareness, mental intention, and spiritual evolution.

- You are invited to become aware of the effect your actions have
  on this physical plane. Are you living your bliss through your
  chosen vocation? Does your "job" contribute to the welfare of
  those around you as well as to your own needs?
- Engage your mind and reflect on how the responsibilities you
  have chosen contribute to the whole of humanity. How might
  you more effectively engage your intentions to set in motion your
  vision of the future?
- Explore your connection to Spirit and request to be of greater
  service to divine will and the evolution of consciousness.

This is a card of action. Recognition of your sacred responsibility
will help bring you into alignment with the purpose of your soul.

Reversed
Has your enthusiasm grown cold of late? Consciously revitalize the fire
of your vision.

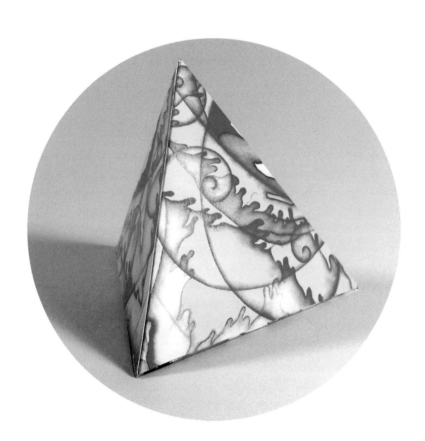

6. Tetrahedron

Understanding • Action

The tetrahedron with its four equal triangular faces is one of five three-dimensional shapes commonly called the Platonic solids. The simplest of these solids, the tetrahedron is associated with the masculine aspect and the element of fire. It is a symbol of action and understanding.

This is the fire of ambition and the understanding of what it will take to bring ideas and projects to fruition. Is there a mission you have been considering or a decision you have been putting off? Now is the time to seek greater understanding and assurance that the path you have embarked upon is in your best interest. Now is the time to take action and initiate movement toward the promotion of ideas and the completion of creative projects.

If you are already actively engaged in this process, this card affirms your decision to act and supports the inspiration and passion that directs you upon this path. Understand that the evolution of your vision will take energy and focus. Remember to listen to your inner guidance and make certain this action is not mere smoke and flames but intentional movement toward your highest good.

Reversed
The downward-facing tetrahedron is water, passive, and the feminine. This is a time of safe passage and rest. No action is indicated.

7. Trinity

Triangle • Mother, Father, Child

Three is a holy, divine number often associated with Christianity as the trinity of Father, Son, and Holy Ghost. Here trinity is transposed to the holy divine creation of family—mother, father, and child. This downward-facing triangle symbolizes receptivity to the commitment of your sacred lineage.

A triangle of symbols from the Maya Tzolk'in embodies this intimate trinity.

Ahau designates the sun and the father aspect of God.

Imix is the feminine aspect of God, the mother who nurtures and creates form.

IK' is the wind who blows life and humor into being through breath.

Pulling this card asks you to open to a greater understanding of the way you relate to your family. Whether it is blood family or the community you call kin, create in your mind a vision of peace, harmony, and respect. Allow the child at the center of this card to spiral you into appreciation of the ones you call family. Breathe love and humor into this holy trinity. Open your heart and offer yourself to a receptive flow of affection coming not only from your birth family but also from all your relations. Honor your connection to and feel love also for the family of humankind.

Reversed
Separation and alienation are aspects of old-paradigm thinking that you will release as you come to realize you are one with All That Is.

8. Flaming Tropicals

Passion • Fire

We here celebrate the vibrant colors and beauty of the exotic tropical flowers called Heliconias. Dynamic tetrahedral geometry excites the image and delivers information on many levels. All are surrounded by flames that ignite the fervor of passion.

Passion presents many faces: the excitement of romantic love, devotion to a just cause, or eagerness to bring vision into manifest form. It effuses enthusiasm and the passionate embrace of life. At times passion presents a contrary face, one charged with intense emotion. Impassioned reactions can fire outbursts of anger and rage, fuel righteous indignation, or ignite obsession.

Open your awareness and sense the way passion is revealed at this time in your life. Learn to draw upon the fire of passion to fuel your visions and help bring goals to fruition. See yourself embodying the positive aspects of passion with the intention of bringing light to the beauty of your being. Engage the most excellent part of this fiery emotion and use its dynamic power wisely.

Reversed
Ignite the passion of delight in order to bring vitality back to a time of indifference.

9. Healing the Heart

Spirit of Place • Healing

The beautiful geometric configuration depicted on this card is, according to visionary physicist Nassim Haramein, the "hyper-dimensional fractal geometry of space time. The matrix is a 3-D Koch curve of vector equilibriums. It is the crystal at the core of the earth." This geometry is intended to enhance "healing the heart" on personal, planetary, and multidimensional levels.

Various places all around our planet have the potential to bring you into alignment with healing energies. They may be revealed through cultural tradition, placement on the earth grid, or your own intuition. Sometimes these will be recognized "places of power" or sacred sites. Particular locations hold potent energy by virtue of their historical and cultural importance and as ideal places to offer prayers and quicken intentions.

Be advised to seek out the places that summon you and honor the Spirit of Place that resides there. Be confident that you will be called to the locations that are in tune with your movement toward wholeness and your mission in this lifetime.

You may be surprised to find that the place where you live holds healing energy for you. As you relax and feel into the Spirit of the place you call home, tune in to your surroundings and recognize how they help restore and replenish you.

Reversed

A change of location is suggested, if only for a short time. Shift your attention and your attitude.

Francene Hart

10. Divine Mother

Celebration • Activation

Here we celebrate the Divine Mother. She is the divine creatrix who abides in the heart of every being. She champions compassion and compels forgiveness. Divine Mother is a vital, dynamic, and powerful reality, honored by cultures around the planet, named Gaia, Pachamama, Mother Mary, Quan Yin, Isis, and Green Tara, to name just a few.

A modern-day personification of this vitality, Indian-born humanitarian Ammachi, is regarded by many to be an incarnation of Divine Mother and is often referred to as the "hugging saint." She has spent most of the past twenty-five years celebrating life by hugging anyone who approaches her.

Choosing this card celebrates the divine feminine aspect of God within you and asks you to activate your direct knowledge of the Self as pure, luminous, all-pervading nonduality. This remembrance sets in motion the awareness that there is no separation—you are an integral part of Spirit.

Take a few moments from your day to celebrate your recognition of oneness with Spirit. Know that as you activate this awareness, you help bring about greater understanding that we as human beings are not separate but rather interconnected and one with all of creation. Thank Divine Mother for the celebration of oneness.

Reversed
Recognition of the Divine Mother in you may help replenish your faith in oneness.

11. Wild Orchids

Something Hidden

Lush and verdant, these wild orchids honor the exquisite beauty of the plant kingdom. Embedded in this card is the geometry of the star tetrahedron. However, something is hidden. Eyes look out from two green hearts, quietly watching and waiting to see what will be revealed. The dragonfly is here to help you dispel illusion.

This card asks you to look within and contemplate what you may be hiding or what is being hidden from you. This is not about intentional deception. There is no sense of trickery or lies; nevertheless, something you have not considered may be affecting your inquiry. View the beauty of these wild orchids and ask your inner knowing to uncover things hidden so that you may gain a broader perspective of your current situation.

Simply recognizing that you are holding back may prompt your awareness to reveal what has been unseen. Your willingness to bring to light things concealed may open the doors of your perception and strengthen your ability to experience the wholeness of the situation.

Reversed

You are unable to see the whole, yet you are content in your illusion.

12. Star Tetrahedron

Vehicle • Merkaba

This important three-dimensional shape in Sacred Geometry results from the interpenetration of two tetrahedrons. One upward facing (male) and the other downward facing (female), together they form a beautiful configuration called the star tetrahedron, or Merkaba. The Merkaba is believed to be an instrument of expanded awareness, a time-space vehicle for multidimensional travel, and a path toward ascension.

Choosing this card connects you with aspects of your being that stretch beyond everyday life and promise to support your understanding of evolving consciousness and universal wisdom. You may want to employ this image to help balance your male and female aspects. You might decide to construct your own star tetrahedron and embellish it with personal symbols. You may wish to learn one of the breathing meditations that are widely available to help you experience the Merkaba as an interdimensional vehicle.

Any way you decide to apply this energy, regard it as a powerful model for the manifestation of dynamic balance and the evolution of vision.

Reversed

This card has no reversed aspect.

13. Dolphin Merkaba

Joy • Cooperation

The geometry of this card results from the interpenetration of two tetrahedrons, forming a beautiful configuration called the star tetrahedron, or Merkaba. The Merkaba is believed to be a vehicle of dynamic balance, expanded awareness, and multidimensional travel.

This image was inspired by witnessing wild dolphins form this amazing geometry. These beings exude the vibration of joy and cooperative play, and some believe they hold a key to interdimensional travel. Seeing dolphins play with these geometries helps us to understand the universality of the messages.

Choosing this card asks you to connect with the JOY that resides within you. We occasionally forget to exercise our joy factor. One message of the dolphins is that joy and laughter are always available, and through cooperation we can share the joy of living. Visualize yourself as playing in this dolphin Merkaba and deeply experiencing pure joy. How can you better express your joy? How can you bring more laughter into your everyday life and share the way it feels? Joy is infectious. Become its expression.

Reversed
The Merkaba has no reverse, yet you may find yourself neglecting your JOY. Use the dolphin Merkaba as a reminder to smile and remember your joy.

14. Together

Co-creation • Balance

Standing together in an electrified field formed by the Flower of Life, golden spirals, and specifically inside a star tetrahedron, this couple joins in balance and deliberate co-creation.

At this dawning of a new era we have the opportunity, perhaps for the first time in millennia, to shift the obsolete paradigm of "power over" to an emerging vision of "power TO." It is certain that the old model is no longer workable. The ways of conventional power and greed have brought us to the brink of ruin. However, by mutual intent to co-create and bring balance, we will find common ground from which to create an optimistic future.

Envision yourself standing in this symbol of co-creation and dynamic balance.

- First, seek your own inner point of equilibrium. Living in balance with male and female aspects within will make it easier to achieve balance when relating to others.
- Second, observe the way your intimate relationships are functioning. Are you living in cooperation and respect with the ones you love? Is there a dynamic give and take to your interactions?
- Third, consider how you are co-creating with colleagues and coworkers. It ought to be more than simply getting the job done.
- Finally, look at the way you view the world as a whole and your place therein. Let this card help activate your full participation in shifting paradigms toward unity, oneness, and PEACE.

Reversed
Remember, we all have moments of imbalance. Be gentle with yourself and those with whom you are co-creating, and move toward renewed balance.

Francene Hart

15. Owl Guardian

Guidance • Insight • Intuition

Owls are shamanic and guardian symbols for many cultures around our planet. In Hawaii the owl (pueo) is one of the important family protectors and ancestral guardians know as "aumakua." The tetrahedral-diamond geometry of this card acts as a mirror of the many facets of your consciousness.

The message Owl brings is one of guidance from the intuitive part of your being. Synchronicity and insight are likely indicators at this moment in your life. This is an excellent time to practice meditation and other techniques for connecting with your Higher Self.

One fun and simple method is to try a bit of automatic writing. A great time to do this is first thing in the morning when you are fresh from dreamtime. However, anytime will do. Clear your mind and start with the intention to connect with your Higher Self. Write without consciously thinking for as long as it feels right. A paragraph or two is plenty. You may be surprised at the wisdom that comes from your Higher Self. Cultivating a genuine connection is not difficult, and appreciating the wisdom that dwells within you may aid in your ability to trust yourself. View the many facets reflected within, and allow yourself to listen more closely to the insights and intuitions that are at all times available.

Reversed

The guidance of Owl is that you are not listening to your Higher Self. She suggests that you reestablish your connection before you wander too far from your sacred center.

16. Ho'o pono pono Sunset

Harmony • Right Action

This card joins two powerful traditions. From the Hindu tantric tradition comes the geometry of the Sri Yantra. Its nine interlocking triangles form a powerful meditation symbol that is said to encapsulate the entire universe in a single geometric visualization.

From the ancient Huna tradition of Hawaii, Ho'o pono pono is viewed as a means to bring harmony and be in right action with the ancestors or to make things right with the people with whom you have relationships. Its intent is to correct the wrongs that have occurred in one's life.

This card acknowledges your intent to create a life of freedom from guilt, shame, and blame. It asks you to meditate on the people and events in your life and to search for an understanding of what you need to know to bring them into harmony and right action. Seek harmony within yourself first then open to communicating with others in a manner that will bring greater understanding and harmony to all. You may enjoy offering this sunset prayer.

> *I forgive myself and all beings*
> *for any miss-thought word or action that occurred in this*
> *day.*
> *I acknowledge that the universe is unlimited potential and*
> *all is transpiring in perfect divine order in my life at this*
> *time.*

Reversed

Do not blame others for what you have created. Meditate on the cause of your pain and then release it.

17. Diamond Mandala

Other Dimensions

Whirling out from the womb of the cosmos, energy is the most basic stuff of creation. Every quark and molecule of humankind and of the entire multiverse consists of tiny packets of energy and light. The Spirit or light body is spoken of in some ancient philosophies as the "Diamond Soul" and is believed to be the eventual course of evolution for humanity as a whole. It is multidimensional and holographic and could be pictured as your interdimensional passport.

Meditate . . . Travel with this image to other dimensions and envision bringing forth your pure diamond light. This essence is the brilliant core of you that shines in love, compassion, fulfillment, and joy. This diamond soul is within you. As you bring it forward, it will put you on a path illuminated by your own inner radiance. Employ this card to journey to dimensions so brilliant that your heart bursts open in rapture. Sit in this bliss and soak up the light. Sit with your brilliance as long as you are able, then slowly, consciously return to your physical body in the here and now.

When you return from this meditation you may need some time to integrate the light that you now contain. Ask to assimilate this energy in a holistic manner so you may make use of it in the highest and best manner possible.

Reversed
Know that allowing your light to shine does not mean trying to outshine others.

18. Faces of Angkor

Ancient Wisdom

Diamond geometries illuminate the enigmatic faces carved on the Bayon temple mountain at Angkor, a vast city of sacred architecture in Cambodia. At this temple site, some thirty-seven of the forty-nine to fifty-four original face-towers still stand in silent affirmation of ancient wisdom. Young Buddhist monks enjoy the afternoon light and the glow of the massive meditative portraits. A deep sense of peace and wisdom permeates this ancient sacred place.

This card invites you to explore the realms of ancient wisdom. Long held secret, ancient wisdom traditions are becoming increasingly accessible for our exploration. The more we learn about peoples who walked the earth before us, the more fully we may understand our humanness. This card encourages you to investigate any tradition to which you are attracted. There are many to enjoy, yet what you are seeking is more than a superficial glance. This may be a time for deeper study, or perhaps it is in your future to make a personal pilgrimage to places where ancient wisdom dwells. Where might you adventure? Be it by book or boat, Internet or jet plane, become a seeker of ancient wisdom and witness how it will change your life. Adventure forth, with an open heart and mind. Be prepared to learn as much about yourself as you will about those who came before. ENJOY!

Reversed
Get up from the TV. Learn something old.

19. Swallow the Sun

Dreams and Visions

The sun is celebrated throughout the world as a giver of life and in some cultures as a god. Both the ancient Greeks and Romans worshipped one or more solar deities, and in Hindu literature, the sun is mentioned as the visible form of God that one can see every day. Aztec, Incan, and Egyptian traditions all held the sun in godly accord. Whatever your spiritual belief, it is clear that our sun represents a psychological principle that transcends time and place.

The vibrant geometry of this sun card invites you to explore its symbolism and its ability to illuminate and guide you. Swallows swoop and play in this solar portal, encouraging you to see a lighthearted reflection of your dreams and visions. Dreams, whether in sleep or the musings of reverie, will offer clues to your internal process. Vision directs your path and offers a sense of purpose, vitality, and life force.

What messages have your dreams offered lately? What progress are you making toward realization of your vision? Meditate with this card and consider these questions. Do not be hard on yourself if you are not happy with your progress. Realize that when you push too hard, you may actually be resisting the thing that you most desire. Relax with your positive intentions as you bring your finest dreams and visions into this reality.

Reversed
The sky seems clouded yet you may find a place of clarity and vision within.

20. Traveler's Prayer

Curiosity • Adventure

This card celebrates the spirit of curiosity and adventure. The traveler is a perfect embodiment of the openness it takes to fearlessly step into the world and experience the many wonders that may come your way.

The geometry embedded in the image was borrowed from Mayan temple walls at Uxmal in the Yucatan. Crosses, steps, and angular spirals combine to create an ordered pattern. The figure raises his arms in prayer at sunrise in salutation of another day of adventure.

As you travel this wide world and to realms beyond—whether physically or in your imagination—keep learning, remain ever curious, and make yourself available to a universe of unlimited potential.

As you embark, a prayer flies with you: a prayer for safety and loving encounters, for beauty and expansion of your worldview, and for adventures that occur only when your heart is open, allowing you to embrace magic.

Reversed

Your life feels limited, your vision clouded. Let the radiance of the sun ignite your curiosity and chase away the doldrums. If you are unable to travel physically, pick up a book, go to a museum, or attend a class.

21. Hexahedron • Cube

Substance • Order • Stability

The hexahedron, or cube, with its six equal square faces, is one of five three-dimensional shapes commonly called the Platonic solids. The cube is associated with the masculine side of our natures and the element of earth. It is a symbol of matter, security, solidity, fairness, order, and stability.

Choosing this card finds you seeking affirmation that the venture you are embarking upon or the project you are designing is in your best interest. Do you feel secure that your plans are in good order? Does the essence of your project have substance and stability? Do you feel there is fairness in the situation? If so, this card affirms your intention to move forward and indicates stability and good fortune.

Occasionally it takes stepping out of the box in order to see the situation more clearly. Take a break. Go for a swim, walk in the park, or head for the gym. Set aside your objective long enough to gain a fresh perspective. Now look again at the substance of your inquiry with a refreshed attitude and realize the order in your manifestation.

Reversed

You are seeking order in a situation that seems beyond your control. Consciously step out of the box in order to gain a larger perspective. You may be required to act in a manner that is not customary for you so that you can break free of the confinement you are experiencing.

Francene Hart

22. Andean Shaman

Welcome • Vessel

This Andean Shaman expresses the essence of WELCOME. He greets you in salutation, extending hand and heart energy, inviting you to embrace the joy of feeling truly welcomed. He is a vessel of Spirit, consciously able to receive soul energy and move it through his being, transmitting it into the world. The stepped geometry refers to the Andean symbol called the "Chakana," which is indicative of Spirit moving through the lives of the people. Similar symbols are used in various cultures around the world.

This card invites you to receive this welcome with a smile and an open heart. Feel how this openhearted energy lifts your Spirit and brings comfort to your being. It may be that you could use a dose of acceptance and the approval of a genuine welcome. This card may also indicate your readiness to become a vessel of Spirit in order to welcome in the energies required for your sacred work. See yourself openly receiving and transmitting these messages. Trust the relationship you have with Spirit and the ease with which you become a vessel when you recognize that union.

Open your heart . . . laugh out loud and welcome the strength of your true essence as a vessel of light.

Reversed
It may feel as if your connection to Spirit is weakened. Observe the joy of this Andean Shaman and feel that in your own being.

23. Mountain Apus

Sacred Places • Earth Energies

This card honors sacred places around the planet and, here, the ancient city of Machu Picchu in Peru. It is recognized as a World Heritage site and is revered as one of the most compelling and majestic sacred sites on the planet.

The green, dome-shaped mountains that surround the peak on which Machu Picchu was built stirred my imagination and inspired this unconventional view of the city. The Andean people call these mountains Apus, which means "mountain spirits." Communication with these great beings and the importance of preserving sacred sites guide this message.

There are places all around our planet that by cultural tradition, placement on the earth grid, and by your own intuition will bring you into alignment with earth energies.

As you are called to these places of power, remember to always go in a sacred manner with respect for the people and cultures of the region. Recognize that as you are called to journey to these regions and feel the Spirit of Place that resides there, you are connecting wisdom traditions old and new in a manner that can enhance your personal worldview as well as aid in the reconnection of energy grids.

Reversed
The earth energies of your home base provide you with all the comfort you need at this time.

Francene Hart

24. Stone Stories

Messages • Listening • Hearing

These petroglyphs were borrowed from a site in New Mexico where some 20,000 petroglyphs have been documented. The step-fret geometry embedded in this image mirrors the glyphs in the rock art.

Stones and crystals are planetary record keepers. They record ancient wisdom and carry messages from other times and dimensions. Sites across the planet where petroglyphs abound are often considered holy places. Humans in co-creation with the divine have carved, pecked, or painted stories in stone that remain today as icons of times past.

This card asks you to hear the stories that stones have to tell. What will it take for you to decipher their messages? Seek to quiet your mind and listen with your intuitive senses. Stones reveal meaning when you pay attention and tune in to their ancient stories. As you sit with crystals, petroglyphs, and stones at sacred sites or simply in nature, recognize that you will hear their messages when you learn to listen.

Finally, this card requests that you understand how learning to listen will improve your ability to understand far more than these stone stories. You are asked to consciously listen and truly hear every facet of creation, including the people around you and the voice of your own heart.

Reversed
You may have missed the message. Consciously listen more carefully.

25. Apsaras Hands

Achievement • Completion

Gracious, playful female deities called Apsaras are found sculpted everywhere throughout the great temple complex at Angkor Wat in Cambodia. Nine exaggerated hand movements borrowed from these captivating sculptures complement the image of pink waterlilies that fill a pond facing this famous temple. Nine is the number of completion. The achievements of the ancient Khmer culture are undeniable.

Three circles offer a sense of wholeness as you contemplate the completion of this chapter of your life. You have accomplished much and realized success in the achievement of your purpose. As you approach the conclusion of this phase, honor the work you have completed and the decisions that have brought you to this moment. It is time now to expand your vision and choose a new path. Each life is filled with beginnings and endings. Even our highest aspirations find completion.

Life continues in a manner that is not always predictable, yet with an attitude of flexibility and a sense of adventure you will see that new horizons and fresh opportunities are always available. Look to your future with optimism and hope, knowing that magic and new horizons are just around the corner.

Reversed

As you resist completion, you diminish what you have accomplished. Ease into the knowing that everything is temporary and that endings beget new beginnings.

26. Antakarana

Bridge

The Antakarana is an ancient healing and meditation symbol that has been used in Tibet and China for thousands of years. It is the part of spiritual anatomy that connects the physical brain and the Higher Self. It is a bridge of light that aids in your connection to higher dimensions. It is said that the Antakarana has its own consciousness and that merely being in its presence will raise a person's vibration and assist in healing and personal evolution.

Connecting with your Higher Self will offer insights into virtually any question or inquiry you may have. The Antakarana may be seen as a direct link between your thoughts and your intuitive nature. It is the result of the interaction between matter and consciousness.

Meditate with this shape. Relax deeply and give attention to your breath. Sit quietly and open to intuition and insight. Let this time act to strengthen the connection between thought and intuition. Realize the capacity for growth and healing you already possess. The answer to your inquiry will come through your ability to bridge the material world and the realm of Spirit.

You may wish to make a copy of this shape and place it on your altar, beside your computer, or in your healing space. Whenever you notice it, acknowledge your connection to Higher Self and the wisdom that is always available through that communication.

Reversed

Have you lost your connection? Remind yourself to merge each day with the wisdom of your Higher Self.

27. Purification Meditation

Purification • Forgiveness

The geometry of golden spiral hearts encourages you to meditate and purify your consciousness. These hearts embrace the energy of love both within the core being of the figure and expanding beyond into radiant universal love. She sits in meditation, willing to forgive herself and all beings, ready to purify her intention to live a life of compassion and integrity. Flames consume and "burn away" all that does not serve the most loving, kind, and compassionate true Self. The blue flame is that which burns away ego.

This card encourages you to purify your thoughts and look to your heart for guidance and support. Old-paradigm thinking and prejudiced reactions have a way of leading to feelings of guilt, gloom, and confusion. Is there an obstacle to your spiritual growth that has caused you concern of late? Is self-criticism impeding your path to your true essence?

Forgive yourself and see all notions of unworthiness and shame being burned away in this transforming fire of purification. Forgive your loved ones, neighbors, politicians, and all beings for the things they have done or said that do not benefit the greater good. Let the blue flames burn away ego and reveal self-esteem and self-respect. The universe supports your growth and purification.

Reversed
Self-doubt and criticism are clouding your vision. Make use of this meditation to regain your radiant center.

28. Piercing the Veil

Self-Awareness • Seeking Wisdom

There are passages and veils through which shamans and visionaries transcend personal limitations and pierce through outmoded thoughtforms. It is by purity of purpose and by the ability to focus intentions that this becomes possible.

This shaman holds a bundle of arrows representing the strength of the peaceful warrior. He is surrounded by blue flames that burn away ego. Powerful Phi-flower geometry aids him in his interdimensional quest. This is a demanding pursuit that will require the visionary to be conscious and vigilant. As he pierces veils of illusion, he gains self-awareness and access to insight and wisdom beyond the conventional.

This card suggests that you are in quest of greater understanding of your life path. Imagine that you travel with this shaman into the geometry and into your own pursuit of self-awareness. Gaze past the veils of ego and delusion. Let it be your intention to move beyond these limitations and into your own personal truth. Courageously step forward and pursue the way of wisdom.

Reversed

This awareness could also represent a passage from this three-dimensional reality, a journey that pierces the veils between life and death. Seek the wisdom and sensitivity needed to be of support to those who are facing loss and those who are passing.

29. Mermaid Hearts

Friendship • Laughter • Play

Seven mermaids dive, swim, and frolic in the ocean as light rays shine down from above. They express the essence of joyfulness, play, and friendship. Hearts created from golden spirals inform the camaraderie of this exuberant play while two turtles enjoy the show.

From microcosm to macrocosm, from the spin of our DNA to the shape of galaxies, spirals exist everywhere in nature. They are the purest form of moving energy. How delightful that mirrored golden spirals create hearts.

This card reminds you of the importance of laughter and play in your life. Do you find that laughter comes easily? Are you daily engaged in activities that bring you joy? Do you connect with friends sharing laughter and merriment? In the demanding pace of life today, we sometimes forget how important it is to have a good belly laugh once in a while. It is oh so true that exercising your laugh muscles is enormously important for your overall health and well-being. There is proof that having friends with whom to both commiserate and share the fun of life aids in living complete, fulfilled lives.

If laughter and play come easily to you, the universe smiles on your good fortune. If you have forgotten how to play, this card calls upon you to seek out friends and bring laughter and enjoyment into your present. Laughter is infectious . . . share the fun.

Reversed

It's been too long since you have had a really good laugh. Call a friend, rent a funny movie, or go out to a comedy club.

30. The Freedom of Love

Universal Love • Unity Consciousness

The stellated dodecahedron is associated with unity consciousness, or Christ consciousness. Combined with golden spiral hearts, this card creates a matrix through which we can realize that when we live in integrity and with heart energy there is true freedom. Our journey of evolution is our journey toward unity consciousness.

Meditate with this image and feel into your connection to divine oneness and universal love. Visualize yourself as part of every particle of energy in creation. Sacred Geometry affirms our oneness and provides us with a language to better understand our place in it all.

Love is the key that unlocks this language and helps us more fully realize our divinity. Freedom is the force that offers us an opportunity to realize an expanded view of our humanness and our place in the cosmic order. Take this experience into your heart and see it as sprouting wings. See yourself flying on the wings of universal love and experience the freedom of knowing you are never separate but are truly an integral part of the divine order.

Reversed
Separation is a false story that history has handed you. Open your heart and let universal love fly in.

31. New Beginnings

Breath • Prana • Birth

This is a card of new beginnings and renewed life force. The mother goddess passes on the breath of life, the vital, life-sustaining force of living prana, as the child is birthed into this plane of existence. Hearts formed from golden spirals carry the energy of deep love to this new beginning.

Pulling this card indicates that new beginnings are expanding your life. Breathe into this new energy and feel the life force residing there. Follow the prana in your breath as you inhale and exhale. Feel how your energy is renewed with each breath.

Picture yourself breathing life into each new beginning. Whether you are birthing a child, a relationship, or a creative project, inhale life force into your lungs and heart; then exhale prana into your endeavor. Feel the evolution of your new beginnings filled with life force and success. Recognize how the events of your life activate new beginnings each and every day . . . with each breath . . . with each fresh viewpoint.

Reversed

Shallow breathing may contribute to the constriction of life force. Pause whatever you are doing and relax into your breath.

32. Night into Day

Graceful Transitions

Magic and grace fill the moments just as dawn is breaking. This is a time of transition . . . dark into light, as the world turns and displays a new day. Owl guards the night sky as hawks patrol the day. Golden spirals form a dynamic Phi flower spinning the blossom of graceful transitions.

Transition is afoot in your life. Each one of us is continuously shifting, expanding, and transforming. Change may seem so gradual that you hardly notice, or you may be poised in the moment between night and day, about to embark on major life transitions. Whether these transformations were brought about by circumstances or by your own intentions, you are required to expand your vision of what is possible and embrace your desire for joy, growth, and freedom.

The age in which we live spins so fast that sometimes it feels as if we are just beginning to understand how one event has touched us when another arrives without warning. Realize that even radical change does not have to be traumatic. How may you more gracefully accept and move through the events in your life? How may the way you view change help your evolution to flower more gracefully?

You are invited to view each transition you experience as another of life's adventures. Allow the owl and hawks on this card to symbolize a knowing that you are guided and protected in your personal evolution. As you consciously move out of darkness into the morning light, let this card be a signpost of graceful transitions.

Reversed
It may feel as if you are in darkness or stuck somewhere in between. Ask for guidance from your Higher Self to help activate graceful transitions.

33. Pele's Summons

Regeneration • Transcendence • Excellence

The five-sided geometry of the pentagon informs this card and speaks of regeneration, transcendence, and excellence. These elements fuel the invitation and directive of this powerful volcano goddess. She presents her summons as energy flowing from her rainbow-adorned crown. At the core of this call is a pentagonal spiraling cosmos.

This card summons you to recognize your personal potential and transcend obstacles to the expression of your life's purpose. Every life holds the promise of excellence and fulfillment. Sometimes we become caught up in life's flow and lose sight of dreams and visions in the process. It may be helpful to shift your attention to that of the observer so that you may gain a wider perspective of where you are today. Are you content with your life's direction? Are you following your bliss?

This may mark a time when you will make decisions that change the fundamental nature of the way you live. It could indicate a time of regenerating, of renewing faith, of finding your personal truth. Conversely, this card may help you realize that the truth that is most important to you is the very essence of the life you are already living.

This is a summons to excellence and the renewal of your personal truth.

Reversed
Your personal truth may not be popular; however, if you act with integrity, it will bring right action.

34. Gentle Spirits

Simply Being

We find within this image the number five and the geometry of the pentagon. Within this five-sided polygon, stars appear and speak to us of excellence, protection, and divine transcendence. The stars of this card are five green sea turtles. They glide gracefully through the pentagons, reminding us to be gentle with ourselves and be present in the moment.

With peaceful grace and presence in the NOW, these gentle spirits ask you to consider the importance of *simply being*. The pace of the modern world seems ever faster, demanding that we accelerate our capacity to accomplish more and more and more and more. Most people believe there is not enough time to get everything done . . . not enough time for ourselves.

This card invites you to relax into this very moment . . . meditate, doodle, daydream, and simply be. Resist the urge to get up and do something or feel guilty because you are not. Give yourself permission to let your cares and woes fade from consciousness long enough that you may see into the moment and feel peace. Pause, and in this pause allow your body, mind, and Spirit to deeply enjoy the excellence and "Ahhhhhhhhhhhhhhhhh" of simply being.

You may receive messages, and that is fine, or with a bit of luck you will genuinely be able to *simply be*.

Reversed
Your monkey mind is running at full tilt. Blow out the chaos and simply be.

35. Dodecahedron

Divine Thought

The dodecahedron with its twelve equal pentagonal (five-sided) faces is one of five three-dimensional shapes commonly called the Platonic solids. The dodecahedron is associated with the female side of our natures and the element of ether, or prana. It is a symbol of heaven and divine thought.

Choosing this card connects you with divine thought and asks you to contemplate the truth of universal oneness. Both metaphysics and quantum physics affirm that we are part and parcel of every particle of energy and one with all of creation.

Consciously move into your breath and connect with the prana force that resides there. Feel yourself moving away from the concept of duality and separation into an experience of the oneness and unity of all life. Breathe deeply and enjoy a feeling of harmony within your being. Visualize how this divine thought will affect your present life. Celebrate the shifts you are making and realize how they will aid all of humanity in our intentional evolution from polarity consciousness to divine oneness.

Reversed

Your faith is wavering in the face of conflict and division. Relax into the clarity of knowing that we are indeed evolving and allow unity to be your vision for our future.

36. Garden of Delights

Surprises

The geometry of this card is a dodecahedron nested within a star tetra-hedron. We might say this is a vehicle of heaven . . . a place to play with magic and delight.

Joyfully enter this garden of delights. Take pleasure in the beauty of this glorious night-blooming cactus and its large white flowers, commonly called Pitaya, Moonflower, or Queen of the Night. The exotic fruit of this nocturnal delight is known as Dragon Fruit. It is sweet, juicy, crisp, and gorgeous.

What a surprise to find a playful, happy dragon inhabiting the garden.

This card suggests that you envision your life as a garden of delights and look forward to surprises. You never know when enchantment, amusement, and revelations will astonish and amaze you. Look for them everywhere. Appreciate and savor the arrival of something unexpected. Laugh with this little dragon and enjoy the awe and wonder he imparts. See surprises as marvelous gifts.

Reversed
You could use a bit of surprise and delight just now. Realize that you have merely to shift your attention and greet the winds of change.

37. Emissaries of Love

New Children

Sensitive new children with uncommon abilities are entering the world. They are being called variously Psychic Children, Crystal Children, and Millennium Children, to name a few terms in use. There are distinctions among them, yet it is apparent that all are intuitive, creative, deeply aware, spiritually awakened, multisensory human beings who carry with them a message of universal love. Their unique capabilities, the connection they have voiced with dolphins and whales, and their ability to use planetary energy grids to communicate with each other infuse this card.

You are invited to look to the future with optimism and hope. It is heartening to know that children are being born who embody the vibrations of peace, integrity, and genuine love. How may you better support the messages they offer? How may you follow their example and become yourself an emissary of love? By shifting your attention from fear to love in each moment, you too will become part of the evolution of consciousness that these children personify. You have the ability to contribute to a future of love for yourself and all beings. See and feel it as already here.

Reversed
Your abilities or those of your children are misunderstood. Remember to be sensitive to the emotional comfort and security of all beings, especially the children born in this time of planetary transformation.

Francene Hart

38. Gratitude

Appreciation • Thankfulness

The golden spiral within a circle here symbolizes offering prayers of appreciation and gratitude for all of life's gifts. Spirals represent the purest form of moving energy; therefore, they are a perfect means of expression for sending into consciousness your prayers of gratitude. The priestess figure sits at sunset consciously acknowledging and giving thanks for the glorious beauty all around.

Gratitude unlocks the fullness of life. Appreciation brings greater understanding and awareness of the miracles that occur all around us every day. Looking through grateful eyes increases our ability to see beyond ourselves and enjoy life more completely.

Choosing this card brings a message of appreciation from the cosmos to your very own heart. Give thanks for your amazing heart, which moves energy through your body so that you may live in the physical world. Give thanks as you open your heart and develop the intelligence that resides there.

Living with gratitude is part of your sacred path. Appreciation of your own divine nature and that of everything around you will assist you to experience expanded awareness and appreciation for All That Is.

Gratitude is such a simple thing and yet one of the most powerful energies we can engage. Start each day in gratitude and appreciation and see how your world expands. As you move through your day, take moments here and there to connect with your appreciation for the abundance and love that fills your life. Notice how much more beautiful the world appears as you offer yourself the gift of gratitude.

Reversed
You have slipped into apathy. Look around and rekindle your appreciation for things large and small.

39. Spirit Kin

Courage • Transformation

This shaman dances and drums around a fire and has called in the energy of his Spirit Kin. Mountain lion, also called puma or cougar, speaks of strength, courage, and transformation. Golden spirals kindle this fiery energy.

We here call upon this magnificent Spirit Kin to demonstrate the gift of courage. Courage enters your life in many different ways. It is fearlessly standing up for what you believe to be true. Courage is being confident in your discernment and ability to speak from your heart. It is trusting that the universe is on your side, guiding and protecting you.

Courage is the strength that comes from within. It is being who you truly are, without fear or judgment of yourself or others. It is speaking out when you believe strongly for or against something. It is the power to transform fear into love and to bravely follow your own visionary path.

Courage is transformational. . . . Transformation is courageous.

Trust your ability to call in the transformation that your vision requires. Find the courage within yourself to express your gifts and have confidence in knowing you can make a real difference in the world.

Reversed

You may be feeling cowardly; however, more likely it is a lack of self-confidence that finds you concerned that you are unworthy. Release your anxiety and courageously step into your personal transformation.

40. Peace Offering

Live Peace • Pray Peace

Depicted on this card are vortices of peace doves spiraling over a background of dark storm clouds. The hearts are created by golden spirals and form the core of intention held by hands seeking peace.

As we view world events in these times it is disheartening to hear of war, conflict, and aggression. Many feel powerless, incapable of action, and defenseless in the face of the outrage. How can we be empowered? Both quantum physics and metaphysical thought affirm that by our intentions we create our own reality. No matter how dark it may seem, humankind IS evolving.

This card symbolizes prayers offered with the conscious intention of peaceful hearts everywhere to shift from darkness and fear to love and compassion. It advises you not to lose hope, rather to "LIVE PEACE" in whatever way you are able. By your actions and intentions, you will accelerate the process of creating true peace. Both your prayers and your efforts in the community to actively live peace and support those who are like-minded will aid in shifting the balance. In so doing recognize that you are assisting the evolution of consciousness toward a world in which PEACE is truth and not solely a dream.

Reversed

Peace is hard to come by in your life. Perhaps learning more about nonviolent communication and the way of the peaceful warrior may help you create a secure space from which to LIVE PEACE.

41. Compassionate Pele

Compassion • Emotional Maturity

Pele is the passionate volcano goddess of Hawaii. Traditionally she is depicted as powerful yet selfish, contrary . . . even vengeful. This card's alternative depiction comes from shared visions relating to her passionate/compassionate side. She is, as we are, maturing and becoming more loving and compassionate.

Compassion is not passive. It is actively opening the heart through the awareness of the interdependence of all things, including other creatures, nature, and the inanimate world.

At our core essence, we exist as pure unconditional love, realizing empathy and concern for others. We sometimes forget this essence or in our emotional immaturity act as if we have. Compassion is the embodiment of emotional maturity and a clue to better understanding our humanness.

"Compassionate Pele" now becomes an example and guide for those who are intentionally remembering their soul essence. Hearts created from Sacred Geometry's golden spiral inform your movement toward emotional maturity. As we mature together we will realize hope for the human race. Let this card be a reminder to walk the path of peace and compassion in every way, every day. Know that your every thought, word, and action has an effect on the whole and touches the Spirit of every other being.

Walk in awareness with compassion for all of creation.

Reversed
Indifference numbs. Wake up to the compassion of your heart.

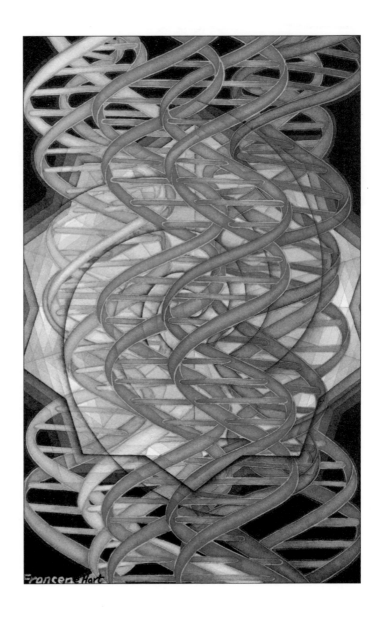

Frances Hart

42. Rainbow DNA

Conscious Evolution

Human DNA uses the Phi ratio to form the wave that spins our genetic codes. Scientists, seeking to unravel the mystery of these codes, observe a mass of unexpressed DNA within the traditional double helix. Labeled by some as "junk" DNA, this additional information epitomizes our highest potential as yet unexpressed. In most humans only about 3 percent of this code is currently switched on.

By activating these dormant genes, we find the gateway to an infinite source of evolutionary wisdom. Decoding and activating this full spectrum of insight and understanding creates a rainbow of possibilities that corresponds to the emerging field of conscious evolution. Part of that process is learning the dynamics through which evolution does its transformational work. Through exploration of those dynamics, we can intentionally and wisely apply them to transform ourselves and our world.

Visualize yourself spinning within this beautiful Rainbow DNA, activating your potential. Draw upon the potent emotions of love and compassion to stimulate the harmonics of your heart and speed your pace of evolution. Each time you act from your heart, you contribute to the intentional conscious evolution of humankind and the healing of Mother Earth.

Reversed

Do not allow dullness to cloud your vision. Look to the Rainbow DNA as a symbol of hope for the conscious evolution of all humankind.

Francene Hart

43. Sanctuary

Refuge • Renewal

This green cathedral is offered as a sacred space and refuge from the world for a time. It evokes the energy of deep connection with nature and represents a place of rest and renewal. DNA spirals connect the peace dove above with the place of heart that dwells within every one of us. The double helix of our DNA spins a remembering of our divinity and accelerates our participation in conscious evolution.

You have much to do upon the earth. Realize that however in tune you are with evolving purpose, however fast you are shifting paradigms, there will be times when it is necessary for you to retreat in order to renew your vitality and reconnect with your sacred center.

Set aside time for stillness. Allow a sense of peaceful tranquillity to pervade your consciousness. You may want to walk into the forest and listen to the voices of nature. Sit quietly in that energy and feel how your mind is calmed and your Spirit renewed. Listen to the messages that you receive in this meditative interval. Allow that simply "being" is at least as important as all the doing that consumes most lives. If you are unable to be in nature, find a place of sanctuary in your home, church, or city. Use this card to symbolically assist you in evoking a sense of renewal and equanimity.

Remember that the emotions of love and compassion influence the harmonics of the heart and the renewal of life force. Mindfully honor the sanctuary of quiet moments.

Reversed
You are moving so fast you are at risk for accidents. SLOW down.

44. Spiraling into Love

Intimacy • Communication

The spiral helix of our DNA whirls around this sacred couple and quickens communication of their intimacy. Human DNA helps connect us to the web of creation. It holds ancestral knowledge as well as future potential in a vast library of information. Also swirling around this couple are spirals of possibility that they have only to recognize in order to activate. As they experience both human sexuality and universal love, this information stimulates their conscious decision to communicate with genuine intimacy.

There are many styles of communication. Simple words may be effective for making a statement or providing instructions; however, when concepts and emotions enter the exchange, words often fail to convey the message intended.

This card asks that you view the way you communicate. Do you speak from your heart with respect and sincerity? Do you truly listen to the people with whom you are speaking? Resolve to look into the eyes of the person with whom you are communicating and recognize the marvelous being that stands or sits before you. Observe both your own and the other's body language and feel their essence. Listen with discernment before you respond. Formulate your words as if they are prayers wanting to be shared. With gentle grace and positive intent, speak your truth in the most intimate way you are able.

Reversed

You may be wrapped up in your own story or may feel misunderstood. Do your best to step out of your ego and gently speak your truth.

45. Passionflower

Appreciation • Awareness

Embedded within this image is the beautiful configuration known as the Flower of Life. It is made up of nineteen interlocking circles that represent a lattice of pure life force.

A brightly colored cardinal, torch ginger, and, in the center, a passionflower call upon you to recognize and appreciate the perfection of nature and the beauty that lies within you. Two hands cradle and dynamically energize this card. This is a prayer of appreciation and a call to awareness.

Gaze at the center of this informational pattern and the passionflower at its core. Allow this life force to activate an attitude of appreciation and fill your awareness with exactly what you need to know at this moment. "Feel" how that recognition affects you—body, mind, and Spirit.

Appreciation is recognition of the divine nature of everything, including the direction your life is taking at this time. Recognize the value of your chosen path. Become aware of how your passion is flowering. Recognize the evolution of your visionary path and hold dear the feeling of what it is like to follow your bliss.

Reversed

Look within and discover ways to better nurture your passion. Remember to cultivate an attitude of appreciation.

46. The Lesson

Holographic Information

This angelic figure is holding up for your exploration one of the most primary patterns in Sacred Geometry, known as the Flower of Life. This configuration is made up of nineteen interlocking circles or spheres and is an archetype of pure life force. It is the container of our cellular memory and one vehicle through which information and light are entering consciousness at this time. Each piece of this holographic information system reflects the greater intelligence of the whole. The Flower of Life is found in numerous places around the planet, verifying the use of this wisdom system across time and cultures.

What lessons are you learning at this moment in your life? What is occurring that may need clarification or a broader perspective?

Information is continuously entering consciousness through this holographic divine matrix and is available to anyone who chooses to tune in to its lessons.

Allow yourself to enter a state of heightened awareness. View this card as a portal or holographic crystal ball through which you may more clearly see all aspects of your situation. Ask for guidance from your teachers and guides, and be willing to look at your inquiry from a fresh perspective. Sit quietly as this information enters your awareness . . . experience how it "feels" in your heart and soul. Accept only what feels true to you as a lesson of universal wisdom.

Reversed
The Flower of Life has no reversed aspect; however, you are asked to be discerning with any information that you are receiving at this time.

47. Fruit of Life

Abundance • Manifestation

This card takes us a step beyond the Flower of Life. By removing the circular boundaries of the Flower of Life and adding another full rotation, we find a pattern of thirteen circles known as the Fruit of Life. This pattern holds complex informational systems and is considered a female gateway. This abundance emerges from a waterlily, which represents our potential for enlightenment.

Pulling this card suggests that by the fruit of your labor and vision, abundance has or is about to manifest in your life. Rejoice in the knowledge that you are drawing in abundance and manifesting your goals.

Abundance comes in many forms, and you are cautioned not to get caught up in thinking that abundance must be about wealth. True, as you find your life's path, the rewards will flow freely and hard times will pass. There are, however, many other types of abundance: beauty, love, friendship, hope, and growth, to name just a few. Let the abundance you are manifesting bring you to a greater understanding of your purpose in life and an expanded view of plenty.

In all things abundant there exists nourishment that feeds your needs and offers you the opportunity to be of service. The maxim "As you give, so shall you receive" is absolutely true from the standpoint of your current situation. The message is one of unselfishly sharing. Sharing your abundance is spreading light.

Reversed
You lack for nothing yet feel a sense of scarcity. Adjust your attitude and welcome the manifestation of abundance.

48. Heart Torus

Intelligence of the Heart

The torus is a piece of Sacred Geometry that when viewed as three-dimensional looks rather like a doughnut. The human heart has seven muscles that form a torus, and it is the shape of Earth's magnetic field.

This toroidal energy connects you with the intelligence of your heart and asks you to become conscious of the effect emotions have on your ability to experience life wholly. Emotions open your heart and can lead to a deeper connection with Self and others, allowing you to feel more at peace and in balance. Emotions can also baffle your intellect and stir up confusion. Integrating head and heart, mind and emotions is the expression and function of the intelligence of your heart.

Meditate with the heart torus. Sit within its dynamic movement and really "feel" its vitality as you knowingly connect with your heart. Consciously experience the emotions that arise. Bless what you are feeling and ask how this may inform what is occurring in your life today. Allow yourself to "feel" gratitude for your very human ability to experience emotions. Honor the intelligence of your heart.

Reversed

You have been too much in your head of late. Enter the heart torus and consciously reconnect with your heart.

Frances Hart

49. Green Torus

Acceptance • Trust

This green torus snuggled comfortably within a nest of flowers is both dynamic and passive. Its revolving magnetic Spirit invites you to move into the green shadowy center and trust where you may be led. It is the nature of the torus to move energy, and the energy moving here is that of acceptance and trust.

Calmly allow your attention to follow the swirling arms toward the mysterious center. Recognize that you are moving through a passageway that may offer insight into the matter of your inquiry. Agree to be open to the messages you may receive and trust that you are guided from within and beyond. Use this energy of potential as a means of accessing your most pure personal truth. Accept that this could be challenging, since many of us do not trust ourselves enough to recognize authentic truth when we are in its presence.

Try to stay in this energy until you feel self-acceptance and sense a message you can trust. Sit with this knowing and have faith in what you find at your core. Gently follow the arms of the torus back into your reality, knowing you may better trust and accept yourself. As you learn to trust and accept yourself, you will find it easier to be tolerant and trusting of others.

Reversed
How can you ask for the trust of others if you do not believe in yourself?

50. Wheels of Light

Chakras • Energy Centers

Chakras are the human body's subtle rainbow energy centers. The primary chakras are seven spinning vortexes of energy and light. Simple attributes credited to these chakras from base to crown include (1) survival and grounding; (2) sexual energy and emotions; (3) willpower, self-confidence, and laughter; (4) love, heart intelligence, and compassion; (5) creativity and communication; (6) intuition, imagination, and concentration; and (7) union, bliss, and empathy. When they are spinning in balance, they vitalize the body and support physical, emotional, and mental well-being.

Pulling this card reinforces your intention to balance and strengthen your energy centers so that you may better engage your purpose and act in the world as a whole, healthy being of light.

Envision your chakras as a rainbow column of spinning lights. Imagine each color as spinning bright and clear. Feel each rainbow vortex aiding you in your path toward wholeness.

Reversed
You may feel a little bit off today. Sit quietly and visualize the perfect rainbow that will help you regain balance.

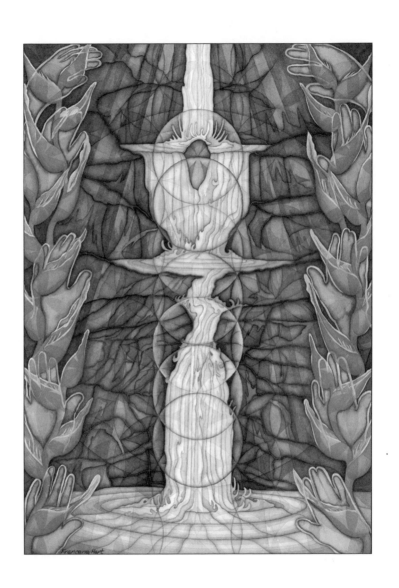

Francene Hart

51. Healing Waters

Flow • Cleansing • Healing

The flow of this legendary waterfall cascades over seven pools. Recognized as a place of restorative energies, these seven pools were used to cleanse and heal wounded warriors in old Hawaii.

The multicircular geometry of the Flower of Life is subtly embedded in the rocks surrounding the falls. Out of this configuration seven spheres are revealed. Merging the flow of cleansing water with these seven rainbow chakra spheres provides an opportunity to balance the etheric body as well as that of the three-dimensional world.

This card counsels you to acknowledge the innate ability you already have to heal yourself and to realize that as you progress toward personal well-being, you will be able to cleanse all manner of unwanted energies from heart and mind. As you stand beneath your shower, visualize the flow as cleansing and rejuvenating your body, mind, and Spirit.

As you observe the flow of water in river, ocean, or waterfall, envision healing energies. In doing so you not only support your own healing but also facilitate healing the heart and mind of our collective consciousness. Each movement toward personal wholeness acts also upon the whole of reality. Each decision to choose wellness over injury heals also the body of our planet.

Reversed

The flow of healing and creativity has been interrupted. Take action in a gentle manner to cleanse your thoughts and restore your flow.

52. Elemental Embrace

Elemental Forces • Synthesis

This card speaks of connecting with elemental forces. Molten lava flows into the ocean under a full moon, where two pairs of lovers inhabiting the steam plumes are revealed. They embody the passionate embrace of fire, creating earth and transmuting water into air. There is an atmosphere of raw creative energy emerging from the planet's womb. You know how it feels, though you may never have experienced it. Coming from a primal place in our cellular memory, this feeling holds the power of the elements and speaks directly to the relationship all humans have with these elements and with Mother Earth.

Embedded within this card are two seven-sided stars. Seven is an integrating number and here represents the synthesis of body, mind, and Spirit with elemental forces. Seven indicates stages of transformation and is a self-contained chronicle for quickening creativity.

How can you more fully appreciate your connection with elemental forces?

You may decide to put your hands in the earth and grow a garden. Water it and see how sunlight and air combine to feed you and enhance growth and beauty in your life. You may sit by a fire with your feet on the ground, watching sparks fly into the air on a dark summer's eve. Perhaps you will learn to enhance your living space through a discipline such as feng shui. In any way you choose, find an understanding of the relationships among elemental forces so that you might live in harmony within your environment and merge your everyday life with the magic and mystery of the cosmos.

Reversed

Circumstances have led to a feeling of separation. Reconnect with friends.

53. Infinite Wisdom

Wisdomkeepers

Whales are denizens of the deep, caretakers of oceanic wisdom, and record keepers for planet Earth. They communicate by means of song stories and telepathy. Whales remember how to travel with grace of movement over thousands of miles, following ancient migration routes.

The four horizontal figure eights, or Möbius strips, suggest that their wisdom is greater than time and depth . . . it is Infinite Wisdom.

Pulling this card could find you seeking a measure of wisdom to help you comprehend a situation. Something does not make sense and you are having difficulty understanding why events are occurring as they are. Quiet your thoughts and allow your consciousness to float in this fluid blue ocean. Tune in to the wisdom the humpback mother and calf embody. You may want to trace an infinity symbol on your forehead or palm, or move your hands in a flowing figure eight to help you connect with this infinite wisdom. Telepathically plug in to the records kept by these magnificent cetaceans. Ask this infinite source to offer you the wisdom you require to bring greater understanding to your thoughts.

If your inquiry is not one of confusion, this card confirms that you are indeed in touch with insight and good judgment, and you may be assured that your decisions will be sound. Celebrate your own wisdom.

Reversed

Today you may not feel so wise. Relax into the knowing that this too will pass.

54. Octahedron

Nourishment • Air

The octahedron, with its eight triangular faces, is one of five three-dimensional shapes called the Platonic solids. Seen in another way, an octahedron is a figure created by two pyramids sharing the same base. One pyramid points up and one pyramid points down, dividing space into eight equal directions. The octahedron is associated with the element of air and is a symbol of nourishment, with the powerful ability to bring together differing viewpoints. It is earth and sky energies united. It is male and female in balanced understanding.

This card invites you to consider how your life is nourished by broadening your perspective and looking at many facets, in many directions, in order to find balance and nourishment. Reflect on the effect of eight aspects on the object of your inquiry. Sit quietly and breathe in . . . and out. Contemplate each aspect. How does cooperation affect your view of the situation? Might patience help events to flow more freely? Remember, at our core we are all love, and joy and peace are our birthright. Feel appreciation for the process and gratitude for the understanding you will gain.

You may want to choose other aspects to explore. Create your own list. The message here is to know you will be nourished by expanding your point of view.

Reversed

An aspect of intolerance needs to be addressed. Expand the generosity of your Spirit and feel how that lightens your life.

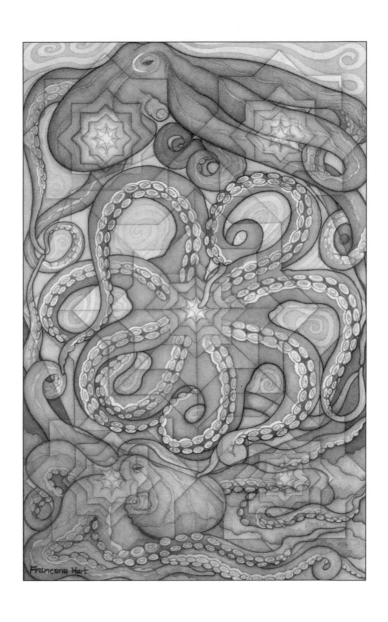

55. Octomotion

Flow • Flexibility

Octopuses are known for their ability to swim with fluidity and to conceal themselves as they crawl across the reef. If you are fortunate enough to see one, it is likely they are doing the dance of "octomotion," demonstrating graceful, flexible movement. They can pull their arms into tightly coiled spirals or stretch them beyond what seems possible. The mantle can take on the spiky appearance of seaweed or the bumpy texture of coral. The octopus is the eight-legged master of motion and flexibility.

Octagonal star geometry inlaid into this card enhances the power of eight and speaks of resonance and periodic renewal. This card asks you to examine how ideas and events are moving toward the subject of your inquiry. Are you in resonance with the flow? Are you engaging the situation with optimism, suppleness, and flexibility? If so, this card applauds the sincerity of your intentions.

Or do you feel the need to camouflage your ideas and emotions by adapting yourself to what you believe is expected of you? There are many ways to move through a situation. The path of least resistance and flow is generally the easiest. Remember, however, not to consent to rigidity in this situation or permit it to obscure your light. The worth of your voice will be made apparent as you recognize and honor your dedication to integrity and express your personal truth. Renew your intent to be flexible in body, mind, and Spirit while respecting the truth at your core.

Reversed
Either too great a flow or not enough can hinder movement. Dance, run, or engage in any type of movement to help aid in your return to flexibility and flow. Stretch and move the body, mind, and Spirit.

56. Above the Storm

Dynamic Action • Clarity

This is a card of dynamic action and fresh starts. A funnel cloud spins, and bolts of lightning flash in dark swirling clouds. Above the storm, clear light radiates from crystal geometry. A figure eight, or Möbius strip, composed of hands weaves around the scene, uniting turbulence and radiance. The Möbius strip is a symbol of single-sided nonduality, linking darkness with clarity.

Every human life has times of turmoil and unrest, times when storm clouds seem to close in and conditions become challenging. You may be experiencing such a time: when sparks fly and tempests rage. Or it may be that someone you love is going through a crisis. Tough times come and go, and it is important to remember the truth in the old saying "It is darkest before the light." Whether it is your own storm or that of a friend, this card asks you to move beyond difficult times with ease, grace, and tenderness.

Consciously witness what is occurring. Step out of the drama and view the turbulence with the eyes of an observer. Act in support of the decisions that need to be made to move this dynamic action to a place above the storm, where clarity and light may overcome all obstacles. Use the Möbius strip to help you visualize how energy moves through times of dynamic action into the light. Envision crystal clarity as the outcome and give thanks for your ability to weather the storm and find a fresh start.

Reversed

It seems that storms just keep coming. Perhaps a change of location will bring you into the light.

57. Icosahedron

Perspective • New Beginnings

The icosahedron, with its twenty triangular faces, is one of five three-dimensional shapes called the Platonic solids. The icosahedron is associated with the female side of our natures and the element of water. It represents the beginnings of new consciousness.

Choosing this card suggests that the subject of your inquiry has been on your mind for some time. You ruminate and question, but you are caught in thought patterns that offer no solution. It is time to seek a new perspective.

Ask for inner guidance from the receptive female aspect of your being. Allow the flow to enter your thoughts in a way that releases old patterns and activates an awareness of what you need to know to free stuck energy and get things moving again. You may be surprised at how easily you untangle the situation once you see it from a fresh vantage point.

Use this perspective to help you see the new beginnings that are set to arrive and move with ease and grace into the manifestation of your dreams and visions.

Reversed

Try as you may you can see no solution. Distance yourself from the situation long enough to regain your perspective.

58. Gaia Grid

Earth Wisdom • Fellowship

Several cultural traditions identify energetic grids within our planet. Gaia is the consciousness of Mother Earth, here seen holding this planetary grid in her bountiful lap. The Earth grid, or Gaia grid, is associated with geomancy, ley lines, and the unified field theory. The geometry is most often represented as a dodeca-icosahedron and embodies fellowship, community, and our collective unconscious. Highly activated vortices and sacred sites abound at places where these geometries intersect. Migration routes and tectonic shifts move along these paths of energy.

By pulling this card you are asked to view the way energy moves and to observe the choices in your life that strengthen or diminish your energy. What brings you to your fullest potential and where does that happen? There are places where you will feel comfortable and those that may seem to sap your power. As you choose a home on the planet and unite with earth wisdom, you will activate your place on the planetary grid and realize resonance with the Spirit of Place. Fellowship can be seen as a means of connecting you through personal contact, travel, or technology to the people and information that will show you exactly what you need to learn and experience at this moment in time.

Reversed
Not all who wander are lost.

59. The Secret Garden

Safety • Protection

Your sacred garden is a place of shamanic journeying. It symbolizes a safe place from which to create a vision of your intentions and to gain a better understanding of your life experience. Ask for guidance and you will probably meet a spirit guide. Change something in your garden and something will change in your life. Some sacred gardens are public; others are quite secret.

You are invited to enter this secret garden through the water. Feel safety, peace, and serenity as you swim in spirals and float at the water's edge. A geometric vortex lies in its center activating the vitality of this card. Climb out of the pool and relax with this beautiful jaguar. He will protect you and guide you to your own truth. In this safe place you can even cuddle up with Jaguar, empowering yourself and facilitating soul work.

The message of this card is of safety and protection. You may be looking for assurance that a decision you are about to make is in your best interest. You might also be asking for a friend. This card represents a protected place where you may more easily connect with your Higher Self and tune in to the wisdom and integrity that dwells within. In this secret garden you are safe and protected by this powerful guide. You need not let doubt and fear cloud your vision. You may be assured that as you calmly intend a positive result and envision the outcome as already complete, you are setting into motion the answer to your inquiry.

Reversed

Your sacred garden may be very different, yet it also holds the attributes of safety and protection.

60. Together We Fly

Growth • Freedom

Embedded within this card is beautiful geometry that was created by the crop circle makers in Great Britain in 2005. It is reminiscent of ancient stone glyphs and suggests a code that, if carefully calibrated, may unlock potential and accelerate growth.

The magical couple holds hands as they take wing and soar above a lush, green, tropical environment. Growth is all around them, embracing and nourishing their shared vision of expansive freedom within sacred union. By joining together in this freedom flight, they amplify their individual potentials and grow beyond the bounds of conventional relationship to a place of resonance with all of creation. Two hawks act as guides in flight and farsighted awareness. The dragonfly reminds them not to get caught up in illusion.

This card asks you to expand your vision of personal power. Envision yourself unlocking your own capacity for growth and then reaching beyond yourself to touch the ones you love. It further asks you to allow all your relationships to flourish and grow in their own manner and to celebrate the potential for mutual growth and shared freedom.

Reversed

Perhaps you think you have all the answers. Shed this illusion. Understand that growth and freedom may require a little guidance at times. Confer with friends and colleagues. Listen with an attitude of openness, and know that when you join together you help create a greater whole.

61. Heart Woman

Inner Knowing • Integrity

This "Heart Woman" is filled to bursting with the radiance of universal love and light from within. She holds in her arms three waterlilies, which represent our potential for enlightenment, and she is surrounded by vibrant, featherlike geometry borrowed from a 2006 crop formation. She stands firm in heart essence and here represents the highest and best in us all.

This card requests that you, man or woman, connect with this woman of heart and your own inner knowing and core integrity. How might you more fully embrace life's potential and live wholly from your heart? What must come to the surface in order for you to live your personal truth?

Be not afraid. Release feelings of inadequacy and realize that by the original integrity of your soul, you are a powerful being of manifestation. You are the beloved child of God, perfect and whole, nurtured and loved. Resolve today to connect with your inner knowing and the reality of your divinity.

This brilliance is fundamental to all beings. As you let your gifts shine, you also give other people permission to do the same. As you are liberated from the worry of not being good enough, your presence will without doubt liberate others. Allowing your light to be a beacon of support and encouragement in someone's darkness may aid in liberating them from the shadow and dullness that holds many in doubt.

Stand fully in your own inner knowing and trust the integrity of your heart.

Reversed

Someone you know lacks integrity. Make certain that person is not you.

62. Shadow and Grace

Contrast • Choice

Standing solid amid radiant geometry, a golden tree being stretches her arms toward the light of Spirit spiraling in from above. She is confident in her life choices and in her ability to both transmit and receive this brilliant energy.

In stories told throughout the world, ravens and crows are seen as communicators and magical assistants. They take wing and swirl elegantly through the scene, providing shadowy contrast to the golden light.

This card suggests that there is shadow and contrast in your current circumstances. You may be required to make choices and act with genuine awareness in a situation you might rather avoid. Contrast and challenge are useful signs providing you with an indication that change is needed. Look closer at your position and evaluate your options. Know that you always have a choice in the matter. Have confidence that by the grace of your inner light and the integrity of your intentions, you will be guided toward right action.

Two singing wolves flank this card, suggesting you view your current position from a stance of grace and personal confidence. Know you are protected in your decision to make conscious choices for yourself and for the good of all.

Reversed
The world feels full of shadow. Walk in the sunshine and find any way you can to lift your mood and feel the grace of your being.

63. Jade Meander

Harmony • Beauty

Embedded in this card is a beautiful, meandering crop formation. The feel of this geometry is similar to the way life force moves through the human energy system. The meandering pathway conveys balance and harmony. Green jade vine and two butterflies amplify the elegance and harmony of this scene.

Choosing this card reminds you to notice beauty all around you every day and to take it into your being as one way of creating greater harmony and accord in your life. See how even a stormy day is filled with splendor. Observe the exquisiteness of any one of your personal sacred objects as if for the first time. Give your attention to the harmonies in music and realize you can experience them as multidimensional. Notice how even such simple observations transform your perceptions.

Hold an awareness of beauty and harmony in your heart long enough to generate a "feeling" you personally associate with each one. Observe this "feeling" and realize you can consciously recall it any time you need a bit of harmony to ease the stress of your day. Walk in beauty and flow with the harmony of the spheres.

Reversed
Something is out of sync. Reflect on the flow of your day and see if an adjustment would bring greater harmony.

64. Receiving

Readiness • Receptivity

This is the final card in *Sacred Geometry Cards for the Visionary Path*. Embedded in the background of this image is stunning geometry that appeared as a crop formation in 2003. The figure is charged with readiness and receptivity. Her outstretched arms and open hand chakras are expressions of trust, openness, and infinite potential. She is a lightning rod and receptor of universal information and infinite wisdom. DNA spirals appear as pillars or antennas in support of her readiness.

This card celebrates the transformation that is taking place in our experience of reality and our willingness to shift from the separation of duality consciousness to the certainty of our connectedness with All That Is.

Sacred Geometry is one way that information and energy are entering consciousness at this time. You are gaining a greater appreciation for and are participating in the evolution of consciousness. As you continue your visionary path, allow your awareness and understanding of Sacred Geometry to nurture this evolution. Let this card be a signpost of your willingness to become a beacon of hope and a guiding light for those still caught in the old paradigm of separation. Remain receptive to the messages you are receiving and give thanks for your conscious participation.

Reversed

You are reluctant to accept your role in the evolution of consciousness. Ask for guidance and assurance so that you may more fully participate in this important time in the human story.

BOOKS OF RELATED INTEREST

Sacred Geometry Oracle Deck
by Francene Hart

Inner Child Cards
A Fairy-Tale Tarot
by Isha Lerner and Mark Lerner, illustrated by Christopher Guilfoil

Tarot of the Four Elements
Tribal Folklore, Earth Mythology, and Human Magic
by Isha Lerner and Amy Ericksen

The Anubis Oracle
A Journey into the Shamanic Mysteries of Egypt
by Nicki Scully and Linda Star Wolf
Illustrated by Kris Waldherr

Sacred Places
How the Living Earth Seeks Our Friendship
by James Swan

Sacred Number and the Origins of Civilization
The Unfolding of History through the Mystery of Number
by Richard Heath

The Spiritual Science of the Stars
A Guide to the Architecture of the Spirit
by Pete Stewart

The Dimensions of Paradise
Sacred Geometry, Ancient Science, and the
Heavenly Order on Earth
by John Michell

Inner Traditions • Bear & Company
P.O. Box 388
Rochester, VT 05767
1-800-246-8648
www.InnerTraditions.com

Or contact your local bookseller